The Songs of Leaves

"What can I say that I have not said before?

"So I'll say it again:

The leaf has a song in it."

—Mary Oliver

The Songs of Leaves

Poems by Carol Townsend

Buffalo Arts Publishing

The Songs of Leaves. Copyright © 2025 by Carol Townsend. Printed in the United States of America. All rights reserved. No part of this book may be reproduced or transmitted in any form or by any means without written permission of the author. For information, email: info@buffaloartspublishing.com

All photographs of leaves by Carol Townsend
Carol Townsend portrait, p. 108, by Nick Butler

ISBN 978-1-950006-28-1
Library of Congress Control Number: 2025934714

*Leaves remind us of the cycle of life.
And that change is inevitable, even as they supply
us with food, medicine, shade and clean air. Plus,
as John Keats stated: "If poetry does not come as naturally
as leaves to a tree, then it better not come at all."*

Poems appearing in *Elm Leaves Journal*:

"Max"
"Apple Pie"
"A Peanut Is Not a Nut"

Poems appearing in *The Cafe Review:*

"Ode To An Old Sweatshirt"
"The Old Sweatshirt Speaks"
"The Wife Admits All"

For Ruth Margaret Horvath

Contents

First Section

Hummingbird 14
Crows 15
Raven 16
Reincarnation 17
Cardinal 18
Watching 19
Nest: A Reversal Poem 20
Dust 21

Second Section

Eight Ways to Know the Moon 24
Email from the South of England 26
Wild Life 27
Labyrinth 28
Jack-in-the-Pulpit No. 3 29
Lettuce 30
Rain 31

Third Section

It Was the Fifties 34
Things I Did Not Know When I Was Six 36
Stung 37
Dance Lessons 38
Derriere 39
Selfie #1: Belonging 40
Interview 41
At the Window 42
A Farmer's Farewell 43
My Mother's Apology 44
Sunrise 46

Mining 47
Batten Down the Hatches 48
Some Things Never Change 49
Self-Portrait As Table 50
Never Far From the Tree..52
Like Ice Wine 53

Fourth Section

Conjunction...56
What Is Carried...57
Facing It 58
Max 59
My Rescue Dog Speaks to Me..60
Torso of Loki 61
Pont des Arts, Paris 62
Transcendence 63

Fifth Section

How a Bad Day Becomes a Fun Poem 66
Gathered..67
Disappeared 68
Saga of the Spoon Rest 69
Ode to an Old Sweatshirt 70
The Old Sweatshirt 71
The Wife 72
Apple Pie 73
Ode to Peanut Brittle 74
The Peanut Is Not a Nut..76
Travis Tritt Tunes Up the Old Amp at Chautauqua 77
A Woman Speaks to Her Breasts 78
Red Pen..79
What if 80
Invective Against a Distracted Driver..................................82
Overheard From the Next Table 84

Elvis 86
Who Says Dogs Don't Write Poetry 87

Sixth Section

Between 90
Honey..91
Underbelly 92
Shattered 93
August 24, 79 CE...94
It Could Happen..96
Because Tanks are Rolling...97
Below the Belt 98
Beware 99
Late November Mail..100
Polar Vortex: First Day 102
Last Meal 104
Weather 105

Special Thanks..107
About the Poet 108

First Section

"The leaves fall patiently
Nothing remembers or grieves…"

—Sara Teasdale

Hummingbird
Chautauqua

Little bird, you are trapped
under the ceiling, perched
on a dangling electrical cord.

Why not aim for opened windows,
trumpet vine, or the welcoming
arms of crabapple?

Why not display your true self,
iridescence of feather, in the bright
light of morning?

Yet, I am that bird with a poem
stuck in my craw, confined by
a vault of my own making.

I avoid finding my way out,
the sweetness of alighting
awash in the whispered songs
of leaves beyond my reach.

Crows

I hate to admit that during this winter of lockdown,
    even though solitude is welcome, I am more and more
        focused on the murder of crows who meet
            in the bare embrace of our elm.

Are their squawks an omen?
    After all, these harbingers of doom fear death,
        hold something like a funeral for their dead.
            Death? Now there's a thought—

I hesitate to think that I am becoming like the author
    who donned a medieval lifestyle, living for a year
        in a thatched cottage deep in British hinterland.
            With neither running water, nor electricity,

so consumed by loneliness, she strove to discern
    the shape of her days by watching ravens, those
        cousins of crows. When I was six years old,
            my father convinced me

if only I listened, I could decipher crow chatter.
    With a child's naiveté, I practiced crow calls,
        intent upon joining their conversation.
            When I finally launched credible caws,

my attempts resulted in black-as-coal wings flapping away.
    I dare not try that jabber now for fear of alarming
        the neighbors… still, what do they offer me,
            these minatory messengers?

A warning of impending doom? No, there are more
    than three gathered. Do they remark on the best hunting
        grounds, mull over blood lust? Or have they
            come for my heart?

Raven

Merlina, guardian of national destiny,
    queen of the resident colony, symbol of cosmic
        forces, has left her prison-palace on the north
            bank of the Thames.

The Ravenmaster, a trustworthy Beefeater, has given up hope
    for return, declaring her missing in action, which creates
        flutterings of concern throughout the kingdom.
            By royal decree, the number of ravens homed

at the Tower of London must never fall below six, or else
    the building will crumble and the kingdom with it,
        or so goes the prophecy from the time of King Charles II.
            Yet, an unkindness of corvus coraxes

with four-foot wing spans remains: Jubilee, Harris, Gripp, Rocky,
    Erin, and Poppy, who continue to flap, squawk and scavenge
        into British ethos. Merlina was a clever raven,
            a problem-solver not prone to roost

elsewhere, nor with sharp eyes, begging danger from passing cars.
    But, I ask, what does the murder of crows who have
        taken up residence on our street, insulting and jousting
            from rooftops, foretell? Is this an omen

affecting the other side of the pond? After all, Merlina is a cousin
    on the tree of life and some royals have already moved.
        Meanwhile, the Ravenmaster, grinning, says,
            do not worry— I have an heir and a spare.

Reincarnation
After Patricia Fargnoli

I want to come back
as that male cardinal
who watches as his mate
drags long strands of grass
into the weeping mulberry,
building a nest while I flash
bright feathers from my perch
in a nearby cherry tree,
whistling a two-part
down-slurred song,
delivering messages
from loved ones
on the other
side.

Cardinal

A cardinal drags a fiber from last spring's daffodils
into the interior of the weeping mulberry standing
outside our window. I jot in my journal, sip coffee
while she weaves this and whatever else she has gathered.

The door opens and closes inches from her shallow,
haphazard bowl, our comings and goings noted only
by shift of watchful eye, her orange beak a beacon,
but her body, a shadow easily missed.

Two weeks pass. Pale green leaves unfurl, the male brings
her food even as my husband prepares the morning meal.
Soon, three naked heads emerge. Feathers sprout, appetites
increase. Soon the trio outgrows the nest.

Today, I stand on tiptoe, peer in, hoping to spot the roost.
It is empty. Fledged? Fallen? Prey for the neighborhood cat?
This has transpired in the same time that it has taken me
to write this poem, which may, or may not, fly.

Watching

She had watched the cardinals
flash into the weeping mulberry,
watched as the female wove
dried veins from daffodil leaves
into the skeleton of the previous
year's nest, watched as three,
always three, tiny eggs hatched,
and nestlings grew.

But the yellow cat also watched,
waited, then the ripple of muscle
under fur, sharp claws embedding
in bark, the silent climb through
tangle of limbs, the snatching.

She empathized with the birds.
She, too, tended eggs, only
to have young life stolen,
sacked by her own body.

This year, the cardinals return,
flit about, search for the unraveled
nest. But there is no weeping
mulberry with its weathered
bowl; it was taken down—
she could not bear to watch,
yet again.

Nest: A Reversal Poem

The next day, I have the tree cut down. I mourn all messages of hope from above never to be delivered. The yellow cat sits in the sun, licking its chops. The nest is empty, feather-strewn for the second year. The cat waits, tail twitching. Hatchlings grow fatter day by day. In partnership, unwavering, both parents busy themselves fetching tasty worms. Three babies emerge, naked and tender, beaks begging. She sits for thirteen days guarding green, speckled eggs. Daily, the bird's yellow eyes focus on mine. I check on her progress, barely glimpsed through twisted branches. The male offers raw materials to the female shoring up the worn, lopsided bowl. I wrap tin foil around the trunk. We open and close the door softly. Their nest is hidden in a weeping mulberry tree planted next to our back entrance. I am most happy - the couriers of comfort, guidance, and renewal are back. In mid-April, a flash of red heralds the cardinals' return.

—The "Reversal" poetic form attributed to Frank X. Walker.

Dust

Listen: on that early morning in Fall, I am digging
       a hole next to the back door, planting a sapling,
             a weeping mulberry   but the ground
                  is parched, unyielding

I spy a workman mowing a neighbor's lawn
       Motioning him over, I say I will pay
             premium if he will do this for me
                  He wipes his face   looks at me funny

says, *I'll dig that hole for free if you turn on your TV*
       He jabbers nonsense about planes falling out of the sky
             over New York City   I think he might
                  have a drinking problem

but he insists   I summon my husband and the two of us sit
       in front of our set, stunned. As dust from a shovel
             arises outside, toxic clouds descend
                  upon Manhattan

but the tree thrives, serves as an annual nesting ground
       for a family of cardinals, well-hidden within a cascade
             of leaves   which in their green exuberance
                  demand a near weekly trim

Eventually, the mulberry's drooping branches grow too wide,
       block the door.   When cut down, a branchlet wrapped
             around a light fixture pulls it loose   for awhile
                  darkness prevails

Second Section

"Autumn is a second spring
when every leaf is a flower."

—Albert Camus

Eight Ways to Know the Moon

One
Launched aloft, Moon Ark's diamond disk, poems
etched into its face, informs the moon about the moon.
Poets have always used   and   abused the moon

Two
The moon presses oceans against sandy shores in endless
dialogue. Poets recognize how humans rub against their own
edges

Three
Wolf, snow, worm, pink, flower, strawberry, buck,
sturgeon, corn, hunter's, beaver, cold. And crescent,
the whispering moon   thinned to Basho's thread

Four
Mahina hears the soft voice and follows the thread,
falling in love with the Man in the Moon,   maybe,
she desires to cradle his cratered face in her arms

Five
A young girl stares up at the moon. Is the trinity
of maiden, mother, and crone ruled by La Luna
she wonders?   Desire.   Fertility.   Memory.
A full moon's face   too bright to bear

Six
Selene's arrival and departure compounds sorrow.
The smell of dust   the remembered cries
in moonlight.   Women watch themselves fade

Seven
In temples, sparrows fail to sing dawn songs.
They huddle under human-built altars, begging
the moon to start *or* stop rains.   To halt time

Eight
A voice travels from the moon, in one giant leap.
Winged things settle for the night, the echo clasped
in claws while earth tilts   *toward the sky*

Email from the South of England

My British poet-friend tells of Lantsherd
on Shrove Tuesday, how children drag
empty cans tied to strings down cobble-
stoned streets to scare the devil back into
the sea. How townspeople sing to apple
trees during orchard wassailing, pour
mulled cider onto roots, knock on trunks,
shout to force out evil spirits, hang cider-
soaked toast and paper robins on branches,
petition the Green Man and the Goddess
to bless these trees. Afterwards, everyone
sits close to a fire drinking and eating
quantities of cakes and biscuits. She says
she loves pagan stuff.

One cold winter solstice evening poets
stood knee-deep in snow around a bonfire
kindled in her Buffalo backyard where
potatoes had been tucked and roasted
until black as night. With a long pole,
she tended the blaze, backlit by flames
shooting into the sky over the city, sparks
competing with stars. How even then, I
thought, *Priestess.*

But here I am, across the pond, on Christmas
Eve, leaving plates of cookies and glasses
of milk for Santa Claus as we have always
done. And, I suspend red and white candy
canes on fir trees…

Wild Life

From underneath the hedge,
not twelve inches from my feet,
a skunk slinks onto the sidewalk

>   *Juvenile skunks lived under the porch,*
>   *waited for the bus on front steps every*
>   *morning with a neighbor's children*
>
>   *Judy says that, depending upon one's genes,*
>   *skunk spray is a pleasant smell, like marijuana.*
>   *All I remember is the dog's tomato juice baths*

It sweeps its nose from side to side,
sipping air. I am paralyzed, not by fear,
but by the urge to sink fingers into blackness,
stroke the white road back to childhood—
let stink into my immaculate home

Labyrinth
At Chautauqua

I am a pattern echoing
four thousand year-old whirls
found on a coin from Crete.
I am a brain-like stem
with sun-kissed lobes.
I am stones, no two alike,
clawed from a field
and set into grass.
I am aged,
sunken,
moss-covered.
I am curved path.
I am a place of solace
where prayers and petitions
are offered with no need to walk
on one's knees. I am pilgrimage.
At my center stands a storm-battered
maple. Where a branch is missing,
a wound seeps a river of sap, like
tears shed, for this tree has heard
too much, felt too deeply— all
those hands touching and
beseeching. Yet, its leaves
still sing their melodies,
offering comfort as it
dapples the sunlight
caressing bent
shoulders
below.

Jack-in-the-Pulpit No. 3
Painting by Georgia O'Keeffe

I'm no shrinking violet, rather
an Arisaema triphyllum, which
some call Indian turnip—
the Indian part doesn't bother
me, but turnip? In the wild,
I thrive in the shade of forest
floors where I'm popular with
ring-neck pheasants, wood thrush,
turkeys, who eat, rather, lust
after, my berries. Georgia,
bless her, saw me for who I am –
a timberland rock star!

I also garner much attention
in the halls of the National
Gallery of Art. Viewers stare
at the spadix, my tender center,
wrapped in its spathe, which I
consider my striped royal robe.
Me, majestic in king's purple.
But, they get the wrong idea.
They see what they want to.

OK, I appear to spring forcefully
from the canvas, suggestive
of manhood. I *am* male, a single
leaf with three leaflets - it was
a lean year when she painted me.
Viewers, you should know that
depending upon the amount of food
I'm able to store in my corm, I can
emerge as female. So, I sing a song
of joy as I touch the sky. *See me!*

Lettuce

Cut off at its base, the head is flawless.
I hold it aloft, rotate, admire, note not
a bug bite in sight. Copious leaves radiate
like petals of an alien flower, swells
of silky, deeply lobed, flouncy leaves,
wavy, glossy, still morning dew
damp. Colossal, a rich burgundy
red at its edges, fading to pale green
toward the core. Bits of earth
cling to tender crevices formed
by ribs and veins. I exclaim
that it is the most dazzling
lettuce I have ever seen.
The vendor disregards
me, says four dollars,
please. Cash. And I
think that there should
be no price tag on
beauty. And, what
a shame it will be
to chew a Rembrandt
at dinner tonight. But,
to swallow such
perfection
must be a
sacra-
ment

Rain

Leaves turn palms inward
droplets caught in green greeting…
thunderous applause.

Third Section

"I wonder if leaves feel lonely when they see their neighbors falling?"

—John Muir

It Was the Fifties

I wanted to be a boy,
not really a boy, but
to join male cousins

for post-dinner games
on the front lawn.
I wanted to avoid

peeling potatoes,
the clatter of washing,
drying dishes, chatter

of elderly aunts.
To wear pants
to church, to climb

old apple trees, reach
for nascent fruit
among curled leaves.

Avoid dusting
furniture on hands
and knees. To escape

from inside. To be
outside. To be free.
To listen to pines

singing overhead.
To plant petunias.
I drove tractors,

pitched hay, collected
eggs hens had laid.
Served as my Dad's

right-hand, although
he may have felt
betrayed once I
discovered boys.

Things I Did Not Know When I Was Six

Bats don't hang out in bedrooms
waiting to tangle in my hair

It's not a good idea to sneak little barn kitties
into your bed, something about fleas

Just because I meow and bark
does not mean that animals understand me

No one in the front seat of the old Mercury
was ever stung by a wasp

Why Mom lay on the sofa every day at 11:00am
with a cold compress on her head

I would have to go into a closet
at church to tell bad things I had done

My most annoying younger sister
would become my best friend

Imagination would make my head
explode on a regular basis

Words could knit themselves
into poems on the page

Stung

At Albertson's Market in Las Cruces,
        a man left his Buick window part-way down.

        He returned to a swarm of fifteen hundred honey bees
            busy in the back seat.

            Two hobby beekeepers in white jackets
                and net hats solved the problem.

For me, in the sweltering back seat of a Mercury
        it was a different story.

        When trapped by a wasp, my parents would
            simply say "don't move,

            but no matter how still I sat,
            I was always stung,

                maybe by the same wasp each time,
living to sting another day.

It is said that a wasp sighting prompts one
        to map the way toward dreams.

        Or,
        to remember that all things are possible.

        Yet, being *stung* by one must be a bad omen,
like, as a child, swelled up for days.

            Or, maybe, the wasp is a healer,
        a female warrior.

        If so, I must be really blessed,
            for I felt her sword.

Dance Lessons
Upon reading Alice Munro's "Dance of the Happy Shades"

As I iron a shirt collar on the old ironing board, I count
        to myself, ***One,*** *two, three…,* and fondly remember
                Saturday morning dance classes in which

my sixth grade skinny, bespectacled self was enrolled,
        taught in the dank, windowless basement of a local
                Presbyterian church by Mr. Gibbs, a middle-

aged impresario in shiny suit and patterned bowtie, who
        intoned, "**one**, two, three" out loud, until we got
                the rhythm right. He paired me with Howie,

a chubby schoolmate who wore his sports jacket way too
        tight. Perspiring profusely, he and I stuck together,
                fumbling through the Waltz, Cha Cha, Lindy

Hop, Polka, Tango. Howie was impossibly light on his feet,
        perhaps so grateful for a partner, that he overlooked
                my lurching, besmirching of his shiny shoes.

Years later, I am again in that airless space, this time,
        shopping a rummage sale. A wooden ironing board,
                a rickety antique, catches my eye.

I buy it, sensing that for years to come, whenever I iron,
        I will be reminded of waltzing with a boy
                who adored me.

Derriere

She said, "You must hide your rear end."
concerned that a hollow back emphasized my derriere.
Ample. Maximus surely.   Obscene?   It looked normal to me.
But, obeying Mother, believing her,   I covered it.
Taking care to obscure   this deficiency,   this monstrosity.
Avoided emphasizing those round mounds,   wearing
long shirts, baggy pants, simple shifts   while other girls
tightly pegged their pants.   Always believing my butt,
backside,   fanny,   posterior,   booty,
tush,   ass,   that fleshy mountain,
to be a physical defect.   For years, I checked
my big behind in every mirror passed.   Red faced.
Considered walking out of rooms backwards.
Until, falling in love with a man who admired,
no. adored,   its perky amplitude,
dimples and all

Selfie #1: Belonging

Reflected in the mirror's perverse reverse,
I see my mother's smile, her nose, too,
and under my eyes, father's bags.

My sister's nose is wide, lips full, her eyes
without puffiness. She doesn't resemble any
of us…she's positive that she was adopted.

From a photo hung on a cousin's wall,
the face of our maternal great-grandmother stares
providing black and white proof — she belongs.

—"Selfie" poetic form attributed to Frank X. Walker

Interview
Woodstock, 1969

They say that everyone has fifteen minutes
of fame. Our mother's came courtesy of CBS,
"The Evening News with Walter Cronkite"…

there she is, in grainy black and white,
standing in the driveway, tea kettle in hand,
speaking into a microphone. The interviewer

leans forward, hanging on every word.
Her voice, quavering with emotion,
does not sound the least bit familiar.

I complain about the tape's quality.
My sister says that I am crazy – that IS
our mother's voice. *What's wrong with you?*

Which gets me thinking, did I ever pay
attention to its timbre and tone? Have I
simply forgotten with the passage of time?

Oh, for another opportunity to ask her
what was on her mind that hot, humid day
in late August 1969, standing on blacktop

near the corner of Happy Avenue and West
Shore Road, one mile from Max Yasgur's farm,
a mike to her mouth, and *really* listen this time.

At the Window

She recalls
        her father waiting
        by the kitchen window,
        astride a counter stool
        watching and waving
        as she drives in

She remembers
        the last time she visited,
        he was prone in a hospital bed
        unable to speak, but open-eyed,
        waving in greeting to those
        seen only by him

She thinks
        that a curtain could be drawn,
        revealing a window to the other side,
        to the welcoming family, letting
        his own father know that he
        was about to *arrive*

A Farmer's Farewell
The heron takes, and gives, life – Celtic Tradition

The morning of the day after my father's burial,
in deep mourning, I drove down the cathedral-like
narrow lane that runs past our farm.

In a puddled dip in that road, on one leg, stood
a great blue heron. Not moving. I rolled to a stop.
Its stare pinned me to the steering wheel.

My father always said that birds deliver messages.
The heron held my gaze. I do not know for how long.
Time compressed. No, expanded.

How, years later, to find words giving expression
to the feeling of being everywhere, and nowhere? Yet,
let me try. This dagger-billed lord of our dark-water

pond stared me down with eyes like doors that opened
onto the universe. As if I were present, and out-of-body
at the same time. It was like hearing each leaf overhead

singing a solo in minor and major keys, simultaneously.
The sadness, the sweetness. The closeness. Then, the heron
turned, spread majestic wings, and rose up over the fields,
its pterodactyl shadow caressing the contours of my father's
beloved land.

My Mother's Apology

Your hand trembles slightly as you stir cream
into coffee and confess that you have been
a poor mother. This, proffered one Sunday A.M.
in the back room of the local diner as we sit

at table across from each other. Attired in your
best blue-gray dress, you were the same age that
I am now. Sun coming through the curtains
blinds me, your face in shadow, but I can see

that you are serious, peering at me over the rim
of your glasses. Waiting. I twist my wrist watch,
twist it again, think, yes, I do remember playing
with balls of mercury from a broken thermometer.

And you hardly noticed when my sister and I
unwrapped the cloth swaddling an asbestos clad
steam pipe, nor later, counted cigarettes missing
from your purse. But then, who knew in those days?

As a farmer's wife, you cooked five meals a day,
rotating recipes— meatloaf on Mondays, cheese
soufflés on Fridays. You spent long hours hoeing
in the garden, sold vegetables to pay for private

school uniforms, stayed up after we were in bed,
a few minutes to yourself. Not to mention your
father dying when you were eight, your mother
working full-time, you caring for four younger

siblings, three toddlers and a baby. Your life was one long slog. I think of my life in contrast, how proud you are of it—college teaching job, career as an artist, large home, gardens, European study

tours. At this point, the waitress sashays by, offers refills. I am still shocked, speechless. Worried what my silence says. I reach over to clasp both of your work-worn hands in mine, and squeeze.

Sunrise
May 22, 1994

The sun traces its usual path
across a blue and cloudless sky,
spreads a golden stain over her bed.

As our mother's gasps become labored,
its rays wander across the pillow,
caress her face, and she waters them

with tears leaked from under closed lids.
She rises toward the light, effortlessly,
following the beam past us, her children,

salty liquid on our own cheeks. Flows
upward upon songs of lilac, forsythia, pine,
leaving her body to cool upon the sheets.

Mining

The wooden desk sat silent, massive, drawers
        laden with forty years of Mom's papers.
        My sister mined this cache with the care

of an archeologist. She excavated a receipt
        for the double-keyboard organ my father
        purchased for Mom, too big for the living room,

        but which she played every Sunday afternoon.
        My sister dug out a warrantee for the Hamilton
        Beach mixer, beater of all birthday cake batters.

        She found the brittle, yellowed, property deed
        to our farm's one hundred-fifty acres, on whose
        land Mom cultivated vegetables for sale,

        in payment for our school books, uniforms.
        Wedged behind letters we had mailed from
        college, there was a note addressed to my

three-year-old self, a few sentences jotted on a scrap
        of lined paper, *Mummy is still in the hospital*
        waiting to bring home a little baby sister—

the same sister who discovered this message, she who
        will most likely survive me, she who will shovel
        through *my* heaps, no, mountains of paper:

        best wishes on two marriages, recipes, scribbled
        notes from students, photographs, exhibition
        notices, old planting instructions. And, perhaps

she will stumble upon Mom's note, kept all these many
        years, this treasured dog-eared tribute to sibling
        longing, and clutch it to her chest.

Batten Down the Hatches

When the west wind straightened
      our dining room curtains,
            my father, like a captain of a ship,
              stormed about, shouting
                      "Shut the windows! "
                            And we did.

This is not to say that he was Captain Ahab.
Only with his land sold and no hired help to boss around,
household matters became his quarter deck.

Hoping to imply that he was shepherding his sheep,
a farmer calling his cattle, but it's hard for me to describe
this urge to protect and direct. Why is this true?

What does all this mean, years after his death?
I loved my father more than snow loves to blanket
earth in winter. More than flowers desire to bloom.

                Outside, clouds are filling the sky
          and light is fading, a west wind brewing.
      I must close the windows.

I am my father's daughter.

Some Things Never Change

I spy my two great-granddaughters at play,
decked out in costly Disney dresses, delivered

right to their door by Amazon, and I think back
to the beat-up steamer trunk discovered against

the back wall of our parents' closet, holding treasure.
A trove of old drapes, velvets and sheers, patterned,

and plain. With a safety pin here, a scarf knotted
there, anything that my younger sister and I dreamed

was possible – Robin Hood, Captain Hook, stallion.
Why, I was a princess adorned in brocade, and veiled,

riding behind the prince on his mighty steed.
My sister being the reluctant horse. Next, Flash Gordon,

able to fly using my cape alone, or, on a spaceship,
with ray gun firing at Ming the Merciless, again my sister.

Oops! There's the older one insisting to her sister,
the younger one "**you** be the magic carpet"…

Self-Portrait As Table

Pint-sized
      Wobbly. Two miniature chairs. Upon me are served cups
      of Ovaltine, bowls of Cream of Wheat. I overhear whining.
      The bus honks at half past seven

Laminate-topped
      Now considered retro. Five sit around, each quietly downing
      mashed potatoes, corn on the cob, stew made from a chicken
      killed that morning. Served on melamine plates, as though
      silence is shatterproof

Mahogany
      Antique. I am covered with a lace tablecloth shielded
      by plate glass. Bickering is heard—who gets to play
      with the metal dollhouse, who first uses new art supplies.
      My surface is cluttered. Until the rare occasion that company
      comes. Then, I am cleared, for sweet potatoes, green beans
      drowned in cream-of-mushroom soup

Maple
      Scratched. On my second-hand surface, a roommate
      prepares hors d'oeuvres. However, she moves out to be
      with her boyfriend, "a real catch". But, I happen to over-
      hear him declare attraction to the remaining roommate

Glass-topped
      Chic. For twenty-three years, gourmet dinners for two are
      served on my trans-parent face. Movies and books discussed
      in place of dessert. Until glass shatters

Table-for-one
      In restaurants and cafes, rotated through each night
      of the week. Mexican on Monday. Thai on Tuesday.
      Chefs stop by to chat. They are family now

Glass/Metal Bistro
    Stylish. Fingerprinted. Foods served on small plates.
    Laughter. Want to shed the so-called happy marriage
    pounds. Except when eating out

French Provincial
    Oval. Gifted by a downsizing aunt. Littered with letters
    to be answered, African violet in full lavender-pink bloom,
    a half-eaten sandwich. Dried chestnut leaves, their voices
    silenced. Piles of poems in various stages of completion.
    You might think that all this accumulated flotsam of a life
    is objectionable.   *You would be wrong*

Never Far From the Tree

Those poets with parents
who lived the Depression

know that flour sacks
can be sewn into aprons

or dish towels; tobacco cans
become berry buckets,

tin foil reused until it falls apart,
string and rubber bands

must be wound into balls.
Make do

I squeeze the last bit
out of toothpaste tubes,

scrape smears from jelly jars,
cut up old pajamas for use

as cleaning cloths, snipping
off buttons first, for a repair

that might, or might never come.
Just in case

Like Ice Wine

A single drop from each grape,
its sweetness surviving pruning,
locusts, drought, hard frost,
dances on the tongue

my years pressed, compressed--
titanium hip, cancer, death of spouse,
yet, every drop dazzles,
does the cha-cha-cha

Fourth Section

"Every leaf speaks bliss to me,
fluttering from the autumn tree."

—Emily Brontë

Conjunction

Look, my Love,
low to the southwest

Jupiter & Saturn align
this solstice evening

so near they appear
as a single brilliant light

but spiral on through
endless night

only to veer close again
in eight hundred years

we too passed
but the light that burned

bright in each other's eyes
was recognized

eons unneeded for us
to meld into one

What Is Carried

It used to be that picking up fifty
pound bales of hay and lugging metal
milk cans up steep barn steps
was a heavy load.

Today, I show wear, like an old,
frayed leather belt, evidence visible
of use and loss. Worn down,
abraded.

Such it is with our lives. Worn down.
Suspended in a way. Prescriptions filled.
Appointments kept. These quagmires
of illness.

Once, the twelve years separating us
did not matter. Even when your hearing
and eyesight worsened, your gait became
unsteady, you were still the man I married.

Each morning, I check the rise
and fall of your chest, fear what
I might find – already having lost
one husband to cancer.

Now, surgery. Radiation five days
a week. Bumpy recovery. Our history,
with its heaviness, is borne by my body.
But, yes, Love, I gladly carry you.

Facing It
After Yusef Komunyakaa

My husband is dying,
one small step at a time.
Hearing in his right ear

silenced overnight,
his left, thirty percent.
Spinal fluid pools

between the lobes
of his brain; a shunt
drains the excess.

A long scar runs
the length of his chest.
He takes handfuls

of pills morning and night.
His eyes dim, needs
drops in both.

He walks with a cane,
living up and down soon
impossible.

The body, like laptop
innards, a complete
mystery — at seven years,

my MacBook Pro, done for—
at eighty-eight, I fear his body
is becoming obsolete.

Max
The Mini-Weiner Rescue Dog

Max spent most days velcroed
to my husband's lap, unless
he took a walk while scanning

for other dogs, especially large ones,
protecting us from all trespassers,
rescuing us from the postman,

the UPS delivery man, any man.
His tongue was like a slab of salami
slid out from a toothless mouth.

He licked our feet and bed sheets, too.
He slept with us, pressed tightly
into the curve of my body.

In the morning, he rolled over,
showed me his belly, begging for nuzzles
along his neck, fur like velvet.

How he stared at me then
through almond-shaped eyes,
as dark and demanding

as a long-ago lover's, and tried
to stick that long tongue of his
into my mouth…

which always jolted me back
to the affair, causing me to wonder
if Max was his reincarnation.

But now Max is a handful of ash kept
in a small wooden box, under lock
and key, as all such memories are.

My Rescue Dog Speaks to Me
Loki, the Long-haired Doxie

I had been in the show ring, prized
for proud stance. Used for breeding.
A great life. But, discarded during
Covid. I was castrated, *how dare you,*
(there goes afternoons with the ladies).
Kennel-ripped, taken to an alien place,
your home, with its new smells, rules.

My needs have always been simple,
my vocabulary, too: food, out, car,
walk, up, treat. But now, when I gaze
into your eyes, I see myself reflected:
a hero, one who turns into a pit bull
protecting you from strays, random
UPS guys, marauding mailmen, men
in uniform, men.

Yes, you of the long legs, a tall dog
I reckon. I do like how your fingers
caressing my long coat. I even love it
when you clean my ears with q-tips,
clip my nails.

All I have to do is stare and you
know what I desire—you "get" me!
I can't help but wriggle with joy,
oh, you of my forever home.

Torso of Loki
For My Dachshund

I am lost gazing into your brown eyes,
almond-shaped, dark, mysterious, familiar.
You hold my stare as I cradle you, stroking
that extravagant length of body,

brindled long-hairs gleaming bright, golden
with morning light. You sired dozens upon dozens
of prized litters; it is possible, I dream it
possible, that you yourself were birthed by stars.

And, if we, together, could return, travel back
to that original glow, we would find that
we are fashioned from the very same dust,

that you are indeed my precious Beloved,
reincarnated and returned to me. Do you
understand? I am making something new.

Pont des Artes, Paris

Locks line the bridge, thousands
of brass tongues gripping wires
of crosshatched panels.

Under the weight of forty-five tons
of *everlasting* love purchased for euros,
sections sag, fall onto the walkway.

As workers dismantle corroded segments,
weeping willows rooted along the Seine
whisper their love-sick songs.

Couples look on, wistful, as though
metal clasp above the this river
can guarantee iron-clad affection.

Transcendence

I cannot help but scatter
pieces of me, leaving them behind

marking certain places as mine.
Each astonishing. Sacred.

Like the path that slides down
the back slope of the Acropolis.

The flattened peak of Monte Alban
where hawks cavort above clouds.

The rope bridge hovering high
over Rwandan jungle.

But when fingers of sunlight slant,
and breezes caress dangling leaves

of the Siberian elm, setting them
singing late in the day

I am driven inside to lined paper
sharpened pencil, the altar

of writing desk. Only then do I
reassemble. *Am made whole again.*

Fifth Section

"Again fall the leaves…
riding the whimsied breeze,
zigzagging and whirling…"

—Mary Cornelia Hartshorne

How a Bad Day Becomes a Fun Poem

Dublin, on O'Connell Street, between Murray's Pub
    and the Savoy Hotel, a pigeon or seagull
        shat down a pale-green glob
            which landed on my beret,
        dripped across glasses, and me, with a single
tissue tucked into a pocket,
    my companions doubling over

which reminds me of the time in Maine,
    when I tackled whole lobster,
        a very small lobster,
            containing a very a large amount
        of olive-green goo that spurted, sprayed,
    finding its way inside shirt cuffs, into my hair, ears,
        and how the entire restaurant chortled

or that day at home when a cupboard
    I opened sent a cascade of recipes,
        greeting cards, and a sea
            of emerald-green notepaper
        to cover my brother-in-law's feet,
he who had mocked me moments before
        for saving way too much stuff…

Oh, those red cheeks. I was mortified each time.
    What I don't want to remember
        about particular types of green
            lives on in cocktail chatter
        immortality.
        The luck of the Irish you say?
    Where's my four-leaf clover?
        Down with the *wearing of the green.*

Gathered

My

house

is crowded

with ever ex-

panding collections.

Containers, gathered

and given, grouped on most

surfaces, the mantle, end tables,

atop chests of drawers; an Apache

basket, tattered but treasured, gifted

by a professor of Art History, the tiny

coiled nests of colored threads woven by

a favored student, the lacquered dragonfly

collected in Kanazawa, a case with geometric

inlay created in an Alhambra shop, purchased

from a soulful-eyed man, a broken-hinged ivory

box with two carved frogs on the lid discovered

in a Beijing market. *All empty. Patiently awaiting.*

Disappeared

Objects go missing from the recesses of my black purse—
        the garage door remote on Monday, a ten-dollar-off
        coupon on Tuesday, or heavens, our Chevy's keyless

entry fob on Wednesday. No wonder my cell phone huddles
        in the handbag's inky depth encased in crimson,
        a cardinal chirping. Why, one would think a ghost

lived within those leather walls, perhaps a long-lost relative
        of the trickster who took up residence in our home,
        blinding us to objects—say, a pair of glasses.

We search and search and search, finding them days later,
        right where we had already looked. Not to mention
        the episode of the missing will, eventually found

in my husband's top bureau drawer where it had been.
        This ghost of lost things also specializes in coaxing
        only one of an earring pair down through the space

        between
        floor
        and radiator
        pipe, only to
        join dozens
        of minutes
        stolen, and days
        pilfered behind
        our backs, hoarded,
        disappeared, never
        to be found, nor returned…

Saga of the Spoon Rest

you flung yourself

        off the kitchen counter   shatter — ing

                your white body

                        now shard-strewn

                were you tired

                of the wooden spoons

        the spatulas

                              laid so casually across

    your convenient, porcelain self

you   a gift   from my long dead friend

      who insisted I needed you

              alas, you will be replaced

    by a much larger,

              chunkier version

                      with no class

Ode to an Old Sweatshirt
Spoken by John to the Sweatshirt

After thirty years of washings
your exact color has been lost.

Bold number two pencil hue
now faded to dull ochre.

You are made of ordinary cotton,
stretched out of shape, frayed

at the neck, sleeves cut off, ending
at the elbow. Venerable Friend,

my Good Luck Charm, Survival
Accomplice, you have comforted

me while I mourned my many
losses--partner, daughter, job,

mobility. But, I am undeterred by
your infirmities despite my wife's

threats to toss you out on garbage
day; wearing you is like being

wrapped in sunshine. The fact is,
I depend upon you even now. I too,

am faded, awkward, with pieces
missing, tethered to cane and

walker. Come, swaddle me, I beg
of you, for I await my own demise

foreshadowed in each thread that
snags, every seam that splits.

The Old Sweatshirt
Spoken by the Sweatshirt to John

Do not fault the ancient Whirlpool
washer for my loss of hue. The blame

for my dinginess lies with you, oh,
Beloved One, who dribbles pea soup,

maple syrup, chocolate milk down
my front, which leads to rough scrub-

bing by that wife of yours, from whom
you must do more to protect me, my

biggest fear being that when you are
not looking, she will bury me at the

bottom of the garbage tote, or worse
yet, cut me up for dust rags, the ultimate

humiliation. Either way, I will pass
into ignominy. Yet, I forgive you, Loyal

Buddy, because I do not know which
of us keeps the other warm during

these cold nights when you wear me
to bed. And thanks for losing weight,

which makes me stretch less, perhaps
adding years to *my* life. Who knows

what I would do without you, Dear
Friend, especially with your wife giving

me the old side-eye while holding
in her hands a sharp pair of scissors.

The Wife
Spoken by the Wife to the Sweatshirt

You would think that you, Old Nasty
Garment, was his girlfriend by how

he wraps himself in you, and you, cut
off at the elbows, stretched out of shape,

disgusting in your daily crust of break-
fast, lunch, and dinner. So tattered,

torn and stained, Suds Sucker, shame
on you for turning my husband into

a geezer. For that, you will not be for-
given. To tell the truth, I do glare at him

when he tries to sneak out of the house
attired in you. When I hear the garbage

truck round the corner, I cajole him
to do the deed himself. Like a pet about

to be put down, you might be consoled
that way. But no, he refuses. Be assured

that I am not jealous for I am not being
dumped for a decrepit pullover. After all,

my skin *is* more lovely than your sallow
complexion. But, don't let him know that

I tolerate you out of the fear, Oh Ancient
Adversary, that one day I will find my

nose buried deep in you, breathing him
in, remembering fondly his past foibles.

Apple Pie
A True Story

There was once a man
whose wife baked an apple pie.
After it cooled, she wrapped it
in layers of foil and placed it
in the freezer, warning him
that it was *for company*.

When his wife was at work,
the man opened the freezer,
and removing the pie,
helped himself to a big piece.
Later, filled with remorse,
he stuffed a small towel
into the empty space,
plumped it up here and there,
replaced the foil, and refroze.

The special day arrived.
His wife defrosted her pie
on the top of the refrigerator,
out of sight. That evening,
before she heated the oven
she removed the foil,
and discovered the theft.

One has to wonder
what was said in front
of guests, or, later in bed,
but from then on, the wife
stored pies at a neighbor's,
with strict instructions
to disregard any request
made by her husband
to ever pick them up.

Ode to Peanut Brittle

One piece is never enough...
I place a nugget on my tongue,
blame my new husband
who was warned not to bring
you, the seductress, home.

Who can resist salty-sweetness?
I savor your richness. My mouth
waters, just thinking about you.
I try, really, truly, to control myself,
but break off another portion.

To avoid your sticky siren call,
I fold the flap into place, tuck
the box onto the lower shelf
of a dining room cabinet, bury
under a stack of placemats.

Do some housework.
Dream about the next bite,
lament my lack of willpower
as I surreptitiously subtract
a small chunk. Okay, two.

Again, I try hiding the pound box,
this time under the sofa, so that
I will have to get down on hands
and knees. Aha! Too much work
I think...

Yes, he did not believe it,
incredulous on the morning
of the next day upon finding
the box, empty, concealed under
newspaper in the recycle bin.

O, Peanut Brittle, I am sorry.
Simple admiration of your amber
beauty, your body so translucent
with its studding of gem-like nuts,
is never sufficient.

The Peanut Is Not a Nut

I reach for a new jar of peanut butter
and as I slather out seventy-five legumes'
worth onto a slab of whole wheat bread,
I recall that five hundred-forty peanuts
make up a twelve ounce jar.

But on this extra-smooth variety lid,
along with the expiration date,
are a series of numbers.

Wait a minute! Consumers are advised
not to eat peanut butter bearing
a code beginning with "2111"!

I never win at games of chance:
a Chinese auction does not count—
the baby blanket won—my mother
dropped the ticket into the cup
and I am still childless.

I toss the sandwich out, smug knowing
that I have just won the jackpot.

Travis Tritt Tunes Up the Old Amp at Chautauqua

Base reverberates up through the floor
and its wooden pews upon which we perch.
Marcie tosses her bleached blonde hair, says,
we may be blind as bats but we can hear.
She fans herself like a banshee, cools
the whole row. She's from Nashville.
Olivia's neck is pumping back and forth
like a chicken swallowing grit.

Cables, thick as anacondas, snake
down from the catwalk. Think *voltage*.
In ninety degree heat. Smoke machines
crank up, lights flash like the second coming,
like Jesus is going to bound onto stage,
but it is only famous Travis Tritt.
In leather pants. Hot.

He spews hillbilly poetry: swilled whiskey,
and the willing women loved too much.
But it's the couples dancing in the back row,
the full-bodied, sweaty contact, the hands
caressing buttocks that gets to me.
Think *voltage*.

A Woman Speaks to Her Breasts
Or, Life As A Bowl of Fruit

At Ten: Grapes
    The pediatrician examines you.
    Averting his gaze, he says to my mother,
    "They are coming along nicely, Flo"

At Thirteen: Plums
    Into stitched and pointy cotton cones you go

At Twenty: Apples
    Somewhere in the Blue Ridge Mountains,
    I throw your bra out the truck window

At Thirty: Passion Fruit
    You were perky, an asset to be squandered,
    right-sized for a man's hand

    At Forty: Mangos
    Gravity wins. I shop for a sturdy undergarment

At Sixty: Grapefruit
    You are sick. The knife cuts deeply

At Seventy: Star Fruit
    A black satin, lace-covered number conceals
    the radiated, dented, disfigured girls—
    you crazy fruits, you

Red Pen

According to Word Genius
there are fifteen clichés to avoid,

so here follows a ~~whirlwind tour~~
of those same clichés crafted

into a poem with ~~the patience
of Job~~, me going at it ~~hook, line,~~

~~and sinker~~. I have been ~~champing~~

~~at the bit~~ to finally write such a piece.
~~(Never a dull moment~~ for this poet).

And contrary to ~~the march
of history~~, I have ~~left no stone~~

~~unturned~~. Do not feel compelled
to call ~~the long arm of the law,~~

~~in the nick of time,~~ because
of this ~~writing on the wall,~~

for it may ~~fall on deaf ears,~~
with me as ~~cool as a cucumber~~,

or, ~~paying the piper~~, or, alas,
~~crying over spilt milk~~. Conversely,

it may become so popular as to be
inscribed in ~~the sands of time.~~

What if

covid variants are players

      from an ancient gene pool

traveling with fellow salesmen

          floating

      in the gray area

between living and non-living

      each carrying a bulging suitcase

      full of gadgets hiding cough, headache, sore throat, runny nose

      wrapped in misleading packaging

they knock on closed doors

      never considering themselves

          alien   invaders

      and when a window is found left open

      they slide through

shed their coats

      sit down at the table   ask for coffee

                    display their wares (at great discount)

                    after a host is hooked

                              they make themselves right at
                    home

          snoop through drawers

                    borrow Amazon accounts

          bother the neighbors

and before you know it their fingers

                    are

                              in

          everything

Invective Against a Distracted Driver

In the Rite Aid parking lot, while craning
your neck to get a better look at a departing
ass, you drove your truck into the sliding door
of my beloved blue-gray mini-van. You, a hand-
some acquaintance, with perfect hair, now

disheveled, crocodile tears pooling in your
eyes, claimed the vehicle was borrowed, that
you would certainly pay if I would only provide
the estimate. When the amount greatly exceeded
expectation, your aunt, your uncles, even your sister

began to call, accusing me, blaming *me,* for the crash.
The Travelers' agent, intent upon calming my fury,
purred that there was no way I could have driven
sideways into your front fender. But,   but,   but....
to think, I pitied you...

                      you rat-faced
          pip-squeaking, lying
                weasel of-a-man
may flash mobs
           of old women with
wrinkled derrieres
           lie in wait around
every corner to moon you

           henceforth, may your
tires fly off
          miles from home,
catapulting you into
          stinking garbage
dumps may an army
         of gulls coat your
windshield with poop

>   may you be
> condemned to hitching
>   rides on handlebars
> furthermore, may you
>   devote the rest of your
> life to washing,
>   polishing, vehicles
> belonging to others
>   *for free*

Overheard From the Next Table

In the path of the solar eclipse

    everything, even shadows,

        turned purple-blue. Snakes

            danced in the driveway.

                Now she has my attention…

        I imagine iridescent scales

    gleaming in the shadows,

the rippling of long muscle,

    but the woman lunching nearby

        has already moved on.

                Whoa, wait! I want to ask,

        was it ballet or ballroom?

Definitely not polka nor swing.

        Maybe a cobra waltzing under

            the thrall of Terpsichore? A serpent's

                tango with Eve in Paradise?

                        As I am
                envisioning
                        snake slither,

                my dining companion
        fidgets,

        squirms, slowly twisting in
his seat,

                creating his

                        own dance,

                of sorts.

Elvis

        Breeding season—
       Elvis slithers through
      swamp water, two
     feet deep, through
    palmetto thickets
   and mosquito-
  infected red
 mangrove
marshes,
on the hunt,
his orange
tagged radio
transmitter
securely
attached,
 a splendid
  success in
   locating five
   thousand
   pounds of
   Burmese
  python,
   eighty-six
    adults of
    which
      fifty-three
      are full
       of eggs,
          Elvis—
            a snake
             super
              hero of
                the Big
                  Cypress

Who Says Dogs Don't Write Poems
An Interpretation

Words scribbled in snow with yellow
ink, a rough translation:

      the wind wafts scent
         of resident squirrels
            into my long nose

              the bouquet of other dogs'
        dinners
        lifts from nearby hydrants
   lovely

            aroma of postman
        sweat
        and, oh, rabbit poop, a fra-
     grance

            so rich I want to roll
      in it,

   but what is that

               I
             must yank

            pesky

          leash

Sixth Section

"The song you heard singing in the leaf
when you were a child
is singing still."

—Mary Oliver

Between

Poised between white and black
spelled *gray* or *grey*
the choice —American or British

but does that matter
this middling color   without color
intermediate   achromatic

durable   steadfast
pebbles on a shore
weathered   mysterious

rich as an Ansel Adams photograph
reliable   tranquil
or   leaden as sky pressed against

Lake Erie's angry waves
caught between light and dark
gloomy   ghostly

like Flint's water   murky
smoke plumes over Canada's forests
questions with no clear   answers

misery   melancholy
akin to ashes   penance
life unraveling

unspooling   like 16 mm film

hair silvering   strand by strand

Honey

a bee's body
        caught between screen
                and window,

its entire life
        spent producing
                less than a teaspoon of sweetness,

not enough
        to stir into my cup of morning tea.
                I wonder if it tried

the tango after a day
        spent waltzing across coneflowers?
                Did it ever attempt an aria

rather than hum a familiar tune?
        Did it die from sheer exhaustion?
                I rub sleep from my eyes,

savor every slow sip,
        and ponder my flitting, busy life…

                my own demise.

Underbelly
Tepotztlan, Mexico

1.
Paper prayers hung from church arches
        sway like rows of freshly-slaughtered pigs

2.
Hooves ring against sun-warmed cobblestones
        as bandits on horseback thunder by

3.
A woman awakens to a matador, his weapon drawn
        her cries unheeded in the fragrant night

Shattered

intact earlier   the expansive

expensive pane   vast plain of glass

is cracked   hairlines radiating

from a small   hole

translucence   fractured

by hard   thrown stone

or small   caliber bullet

breaking   a sweat

the workman   crisscrosses

tape as black as coal   random lines

lanes resembling   assembling

a Mondrian painting   or

broken   trust

August 24, 79 CE
From Pliny the Younger's Writings and a Poet's Musings About the Wealthy Man

In the seventh hour after sunrise,
Pliny the Younger's mother points
to "a cloud of unusual size and shape"

> I fret over the rising plume, but refuse
> to leave my fields, orchards and vineyards,
> lands stretching northwest from city walls.
> Only as lapilli begin showering down
> do I hasten, with my most trusted slave,
> into a nearby cryptoporticus

By one o'clock, ash and pumice coughed
from Vesuvius land six miles away.
By five o'clock, roofs collapse under its weight

> We will be safe here from volcanic wrath,
> not like the man with scarf-wrapped nose
> in mid-sprint. I grieve for prized horses
> left behind, even the dog who will die,
> lips curled back, its collar and chain intact

Rocks, at speed of fifty miles per second,
hurtle down. The sun is blocked. No daylight.
Some neighbors rush toward the harbor…

> Thanks be to Apollo that my slave followed,
> a comfort now as we crouch side-by-side.
> I will richly reward him when we escape
> from this underground cell. But now, each breath
> we take   is   becoming   labored.
> Who will be heir   to my harvest?

...the eruption column grows taller.
Surges of more than five hundred degrees
steal breath from lungs

        Not even fine woolen garments
                can protect us   and me,   without
                    a proper burial befitting my elevated
          status.

                Never will Vesuvius Gate necropolis
                    hold   my ashes.

            Instead,

                      ash

                will

                              cradle

                us

It Could Happen

because it has, in Squirrel Hill,
        home to a dozen synagogues.
                Heralded by sirens,

shock,   dread,   for our country,
that neighborhoods could come to this—
        the soft target of Shabbat

              shattered in October 2018
by a man, *the* man,
        from apartment number one

        whom no neighbor knew
     nor remembered his name.
Empty beer bottles outside.

        No guests.   He lived alone
            after his grandfather died.
     He seemed normal.

Yet all those guns,   and hate,
        on the other side of thin walls…

     hold fast to the tree of life.

Because Tanks are Rolling

into Kyiv, our dog growled
at a neighbor's terrier, lunged
with bared teeth at leash's end

warning that this small patch
of earth considered ***homeland***,
a slight quarter acre of suburbia

full of familiar smells, squirrels,
rabbits, crickets and his humans,
was *his-land.* The other dog

was clearly covetous, might
possibly have lived on this plot
in a past life, but withdrew quickly.

Unlike others of the two- legged
variety, in its desire to possess,
did not invade, maim,

    kill   *destroy*

        destroy

                destroy

Below the Belt
Inspired by poisoning of Alexi Navalny

The last place
to expect
poison
is in one's
underwear

whether it be
white cotton
briefs
or Victoria Secret
satin and lace

the toxin need not be
Novichok
planted by
a Russian operative
there is one

as pernicious--
revenge porn
sowed by one's
supposed
sweetheart

in ultimate betrayal
the poisoned
go on
living
a half-life

Beware

of advertising
        sporting smiling babies,
        spandex-clad beauties,
        and voice-overs extolling
                the myriad benefits
                of a particular drug,
                likely ending in an "e" or "m"

or the e-mail promoting
        a three thousand year-old tonic
        for losing weight,
        manufactured in Raleigh,
                that proclaims a loss
                of thirty-three pounds
                in *just* twenty-four days

note that in both cases, the number
        of grins can be proportionate
        to the fine print of suffering:
        gastroenteritis, hepatic disease,
                serious blood clots,
                low white blood cell counts
                that could *lead to*
                death

Late November Mail

Scattered among the pile
        of ads for mufflers, tires,
        and political endorsements
        are pleas from agencies:

Thirty thousand children
        die every day in Africa,
        three cents can save one.
        One dollar ninety-eight

feeds a hungry homeless
        person in the cold of winter.
        I pry off the small coins
        so tightly affixed.

At the bottom of the heap,
        a heavy envelope addressed
        with handsome script
        proclaiming "life without limits",

bragging of around-the-clock
        access to a team ready to book
        restaurant reservations,
        exclusive itineraries—

complete lifestyle management—
        own this special, luxury credit card
        engineered with stainless steel
        front and carbon back,

for durability *and* distinction.
        But what about the coins of copper,
        nickel, zinc that burn in my pocket?
        What about the children who starve,

only leaves for dinner, their bellies
        bloated, blank eyes staring out
        over the lip of recycle bins....
        the unbearable weight

Polar Vortex: First Day

December 2023, Buffalo New York

Forty-four people will lose their lives.

The sun revolts, rises pale. Temperatures collapse.
        Not a lovely diamond dusting, but driving snow slices
        sideways

more like swarming locusts. Was this storm forecast?
        It builds, blurring, blotting out the view

To peer out through the storm door is like looking through

astigmatic eyes. Except for the collection of clots

Conquest, or surrender comes to mind.
Hearts hurt down to the endocardium—
        didn't we know that it was was coming

Flakes accumulating atop hedges block windows,
        pane by pane. In darkening rooms, orchid buds stay
        tightly closed, like clenched fists

The squall moans, frenzied. Waves of grey, deepening into
black,

        smudge everything. Eight foot drifts block doors.

        Winds whip the bark off sycamores

The blizzard fails to cease. Perhaps forming into poems

    Coming coming   *coming*

Last Meal

Why didn't Billy Ray Irick, convicted killer
of a seven-year-old, choose the standard last meal?
Steak cooked medium-rare, eggs over easy, toast

with butter and jelly, milk, coffee, and juice.
Given the twenty-dollar limit, he ordered a super
deluxe burger, onion rings, and large Pepsi.

Evidently, Billy was not concerned with cholesterol
nor calories. However, this gets me thinking...
what would I choose for my last meal?

Hmm. A filet mignon, well-done from Russell's?
Too expensive. How about a foot-long hot dog
with everything on it? And baked beans,

corn on the cob slathered in butter. A milkshake
for dessert? Whoa. *Might give me gas...*
A big slab of lemon meringue pie, the kind

that makes one's mouth pucker, its perfect peaks
browned with little beads of melted sugar?
Not possible because my Mom is long dead.

OK. A perfectly ripe peach, its skin so velvety,
juice tasting of summer running down chins.
Nope. It's winter and peach season is over.

The truth is I will not know the exact hour
of my last meal. Will I be eating breakfast
at the kitchen table?

Or sipping a cafe mocha latte on an ordinary day?
Will I be terminal, receiving food through a tube?
Maybe it's better to just get the three-drug injection...

Weather

If words were snowflakes,
        I would be knee-deep
        in them, write a novel

But I compose
        poems, choose few words,
         labor to reveal pavement
        hidden beneath

With shovel
        I remove snow
        from sidewalks for paperboy
        and mailman

I bend
        to examine leaves
        frozen fast against icy earth
        their songs long silenced

With pen
        I arrange words on the page,
        attempt to clear a path
        between you and me

Special Thanks

To the Lake Erie Poets, Ann, Anne, Elaine, Jennifer, Joan, and Judy for their support over the years, for the poetry workshops taken at the Chautauqua Writers' Center, to Marge Norris for introducing me to the world of poetry, to Irene Sipos for her keen editor's eye, to ryki zuckerman who has assisted greatly in getting my poems out into the public, to my kind publisher, Len Kagelmacher, to the late Thomas Sist, who encouraged me to write in the first place, and to my beloved husband, John Cofield, for his patience and enthusiasm.

About the Poet

Photo by Nick Butler

Carol Townsend received her B.S. in Art from Nazareth College of Rochester and her M.F.A. in Applied Design in Ceramics from Ohio University. She served as an Associate Professor of Art & Design and former chair of the Design Department at Buffalo State University prior to her retirement. As an award-winning ceramicist and mixed media artist, her works are represented in numerous collections. She has been a frequent participant in the Chautauqua Writers' Center poetry workshops and served on the board of the Friends of the Chautauqua Writers' Center for a number of years.

Her poems have appeared in the journals *Voices de la Luna*, *Sow's Ear*, *The Healing Muse*, *The Cafe Review*, and the *Elm Leaves Journal*, as well as in the *Buffalo News*. She has been an invited reader in *The Gray Hair*, *Rooftop*, *Wordflight*, *Red Door*, *Literary Cafe Series*, *A Musical Feast*, *The Buffalo Corner Reading Series*, and the *Emanuel Fried Drop Hammer Student Reading Series*. One of her poems was selected for the public art project, *BuffLit:On the Move*, sponsored by Just Buffalo Literary Center and the Niagara Frontier Transportation Authority.

Her chapbook, *A Cinder In My Knee*, was published in 2016 and her full length book, *The Color of Shadows*, in 2019, both by Buffalo Arts Publishing.

An avid gardener and photographer, she resides with her husband, John and mini-dachshund, Loki, in Snyder, New York.

www.ingramcontent.com/pod-product-compliance
Lightning Source LLC
Chambersburg PA
CBHW040252090526
44586CB00041B/2783